Other books by

HAMISH MACINNES

CALL-OUT

CLIMB TO THE LOST WORLD

LOOK BEHIND THE RANGES

HIGH DRAMA

SCOTTISH CLIMBS 1

SCOTTISH CLIMBS 2

WEST HIGHLAND WALKS 1

WEST HIGHLAND WALKS 2

WEST HIGHLAND WALKS 3

HIGHLAND WALKS

SCOTTISH WINTER CLIMBS

BEYOND THE RANGES

THE PRICE OF ADVENTURE

INTERNATIONAL MOUNTAIN RESCUE HANDBOOK

SWEEP SEARCH

MY SCOTLAND

DEATH REEL (fiction)

Previous Photograph
Achnacon and Lower Glencoe.

LAND OF MOUNTAIN AND MIST

ACKNOWLEDGEMENTS

I should like to thank all who supported me with this book, especially Graeme Hunter for his invaluable advice and Philip Massie of Masterscan for his technical expertise; also the printers, who exercised commendable patience for one unfamiliar with the labyrinth of their craft. Lastly, I am indebted to the Highlands of Scotland which provided such a plethora of colour, light and shadow.

HMI

1989

First published in Great Britain
by Glencoe Productions Ltd.
Glencoe Argyll, Scotland PA39 4LA.
Copyright © 1989 Hamish MacInnes

Reproduction by Masterscan, Inverness
Typeset and printed in Scotland by
Pillans & Wilson, Edinburgh
Bound by Hunter & Foulis, Edinburgh

ISBN 0 9514380 0 X Land of Mountain and Mist. (hbk)

ABOUT THIS BOOK

Scotland is a unique country and even in this the 20th century, it still retains a mystical quality, especially in the Highlands and Islands. The photographs in this book are mainly about this area, a land of mountain and mist, of heather and a seaboard fragmented by the relentless Atlantic Ocean.

I have tried to portray a cross section of the superb scenery, of the glens and hills in their many moods and of an area which is fundamentally the most unspoiled part of Europe. There are few places left where you can walk all day and not have to cross a single fence, where the eagle circles high above and red deer run wild in the heather.

There are of course penalties for such pleasures; the midge, small creature with a large summer appetite, and often hand in hand comes the rain. Spring is usually the time to see the Highlands at its best, when there are still remnants of snow on the summits and when the day never wants to end. It is a country to savour at your leisure and a place that you will always fondly remember.

CAPTIONS AND VERSE

1. The remote Garbh Coire, Beinn a'Bhuird, Cairngorms. . . . . GREY GRANITE

2. The village of Shieldaig, Torridon with the gneiss exposure on the north side of the loch. . . . . ROCK DESERT

3. Am Buachaille from Sandwood Bay, northwards there is no land until Greenland. . . . . HERDSMAN OF THE OCEAN

4. The Cobbler, Arrochar. This is a popular rock playground for Glasgow climbers. . . . . . THE COBBLER

5. The Pap of Glencoe with Ballachulish and the Burial Isle. . . . . MACIAIN OF GLENCOE

6. Stac Polly from Knockanrock. . . . . EVENSONG

7. Coire Gabhail, the Lost Valley, Glencoe.
   It was here that the MacDonalds used to hide stolen or reived cattle, the name means the Coire of the Capture. . . INSOMNIA

8. Sgurr an Fhidhleir beyond Loch Lurgainn. . . . . THE SGURR

9. Hirta, St Kilda, from Boreray with the gannetry of Stac Lee in the foreground. St Kilda is fifty miles west of the Outer Hebrides and it was evacuated in 1930. One of its ministers, the Rev. John MacKay used to preach protracted sermons. ST KILDA

10. Eilean Fhionnan, the burial isle on Loch Shiel by Dalelia. A place of great tranquillity. . . . . I TAKE MY REST

11. A golden eagle. . . . . HIGH PERCEPTION

12. The great cliffs of Bheinn Bhan, Applecross. . . . . FREEDOM

13. Looking westwards over Loch Garry towards Knoydart. . . . . WHEN DARKNESS FALLS

14. The Aonach Eagach Ridge, Glencoe. . . . . ZIG-ZAGGING THROUGH THE HEAVENS

15. The village of Diabaig, Loch Torridon with Liathach behind. . . . . NICE

16. The Island of Eigg and the Sgurr. . . . . AN ENCHANTED ISLAND

17. The Clach Leathad group from the Moor of Rannoch. . . . . MOOR OF RANNOCH

18. The Innaccessible Pinnacle, Sgurr Dearg, Cuillin of Skye. . . . . THE PINNACLE

19. Ardnamurchan Point. The Point of the Great Ocean. . . . . . . THE POINT OF THE GREAT OCEAN

20. No. 2 Gully, Ben Nevis. The summit is to the left of the figures. . . . . . . EXPECTATIONS HIGH

21. Ben Lomond from Tarbet. . . . . SUMMER DAYS

22. Stob Coire nam Beith, Glencoe. . . . . ELEPHANT HEAD

23. Buachaille Etive Mor in Summer. . . . . THE GREAT HERDSMAN

24. Lazy beds and the Cuillin from near Carbost. (front cover) . . . . LAZYBEDS

25. Loch Torridon from the north Applecross shore. . . . . THE LITTLE RED-ROOFED HOUSE

26. Loch Duich and the peaks of Kintail. . . . . FADING TO INFINITY

27. Sgurr nan Gillean and its minions from near Sligachan. . . . . THE CUILLIN

28. The peaks of Glencoe from Beinn a'Bheithir. . . . . AN ELEVATED PLACE

29. An Teallach from the Road of Destitution. . . . . COLD REALITY

30. Rubha nan Clach from Ullinish. . . . . TRANSIENT

CAPTIONS AND VERSE

1. **GREY GRANITE**

*R*OCK BURSTING THROUGH THE HEATHERY GRASS,
GREY GRANITE SLABS AND SLIPPERY SUMMITS,
DISCHARGING MEMORIES OF THE PAST,
INVADING DISTANT CORNERS OF MY MIND,
BECKONING MY NEXT TRESPASS.

The remote Garbh Coire, Beinn a'Bhuird, Cairngorms.

2. **ROCK DESERT**

Shieldaig, oasis in a rocky desert,
hugging loch torridon's wavy edge.
on quiet days i warm to your memory,
from distant shores.

The village of Shieldaig, Torridon with the gneiss exposure on the north side of the loch.

3.   HERDSMAN OF THE OCEAN

WITH THE ELEMENTS YOU COMPETE,

WILD SURF SNAPPING AT YOUR SANDSTONE FEET.

UNMOVED BY TIDAL MOTION,

AM BUACHAILLE, HERDSMAN OF THE OCEAN.

Am Buachaille from Sandwood Bay, northwards there is no land until Greenland.

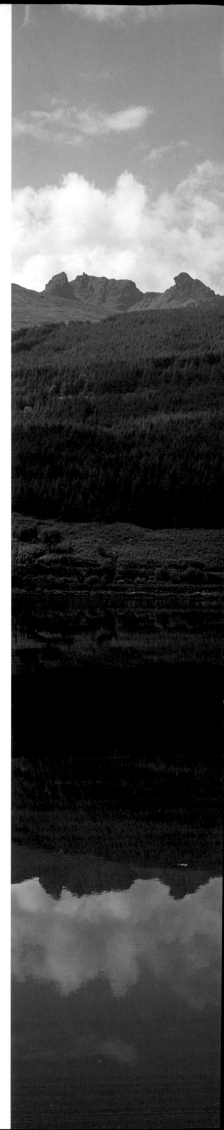

4. **THE COBBLER**

*B*ETWEEN THE HILLS OF GREEN,

BROWN AND DEEP PURPLE,

PEAKED THE CRAGGY SUMMIT

OF THE COBBLER,

SHARP IN THE SEPTEMBER SKY.

A VISION WHICH HAS TEMPTED

MANY A CLIMBER,

DEMANDING HIS ZEST.

THIS ALL REFLECTED IN

THE STILL WATERS OF LOCH LONG,

AS THE LATE AFTERNOON SUN,

SOFT AND LOW,

CAST LONG BROWN SHADOWS

AND HEADED WEST.

The Cobbler, Arrochar. This is a popular rock playground for Glasgow climbers.

5.   **MACIAIN OF GLENCOE**

(From the song MacIain of Glencoe)

*Y*ET STILL MY LONELY SPIRIT SOARS

AMID THE MOUNTAINS AND THE GLEN,

FROM MY ANCESTRAL BURIAL GROUND,

I AM MACIAIN.

THE NAME MACDONALD ECHOES STILL,

WITHIN THE HEARTS OF HIGHLAND MEN,

MY RESTLESS SOUL WILL NEVER SLEEP,

I AM MACIAIN.

The Pap of Glencoe with Ballachulish and the Burial Isle.

6. **EVENSONG**

THOSE WHO HAVE EXPERIENCED
ONE FOOT IN HEAVENS' DOOR,
HOLD THE MEMORY OF THAT JOURNEY,
TILL THEY TRAVEL IT ONCE MORE.
THEY SAY PEACEFULNESS WAS BECKONING
FROM A PLACE OF TEMPTING BLISS.
WOULD THAT THE SUNSET OF MY LIFE
COULD BE AS BEAUTIFUL AS THIS.

Stac Polly from Knockanrock.

7.   **INSOMNIA**

TRYING TO SLEEP,

LISTLESS, SLEEP—WAKING,

DREAM—THINKING

OF FANTASY, REALITY,

FUTURE AND PAST,

TUMBLING IN A SPHERE,

DELICATELY WOVEN

SOMEWHERE

BETWEEN THERE AND HERE.

Coire Gabhail, the Lost Valley, Glencoe.

It was here that the MacDonalds used to hide stolen or reived cattle, the name means the Coire of the Capture.

8.   THE SGURR

GLACIERS MOVED,

GOUGING THE EARTH,

LOWERING LANDSCAPES

BUT NOT YOUR

TORRIDONIAN SANDSTONE CORE.

Sgurr an Fhidhleir beyond Loch Lurgainn.

9.   **ST KILDA**

*F*OR TWO THOUSAND YEARS THEY SURVIVED,

ON SEABIRDS, FISH AND RELIGION MOST HIGH,

THE LATTER, EACH DAY AND THREE TIMES ON SUNDAY,

SERVED UP BY THE REVEREND MACKAY.

Hirta, St Kilda, from Boreray with the gannetry of Stac Lee in the foreground. St Kilda is fifty miles west of the Outer Hebrides and it was evacuated in 1930. One of its ministers, the Rev. John MacKay used to preach protracted sermons.

10.   I TAKE MY REST

*S*UMMER BLOOMS IN COLOUR THAT ABOUNDS.

BENEATH SOME LADEN BOUGHS I TAKE MY REST,

THE BIRDS AND BEES POUR FORTH THEIR SOOTHING SOUNDS,

THE SYMPHONY OF SUMMER IN MY BREAST.

Eilean Fhionnan, the burial isle on Loch Shiel by Dalelia. A place of great tranquillity.

11.   HIGH PERCEPTION

I WONDER, NOBLE-HEADED BIRD,

WHAT MOVEMENT YOUR CLEAR EYE OBSERVES,

WHILE YOU IN YOUR EXALTED PLACE,

SIT STILL AS DEATH.

A golden eagle.

12. FREEDOM

From the song, "Shout it from the Mountainside".

*N*O MORE YOUR OPINIONS HIDE,

SHOUT IT FROM THE MOUNTAINSIDE,

LET THEM KNOW THE WORLD OUTSIDE,

STILL CARES ABOUT THEIR FREEDOM.

The great cliffs of Bheinn Bhan, Applecross.

13.   **WHEN DARKNESS FALLS**

WHEN DARKNESS FALLS AND SILHOUETTES THE TREES;
SHADOWS ON THE LOCH GROW DEEP AND STILL.
I'M THANKFUL I CAN WANDER WHERE I PLEASE,
AND RECALL THESE SCENES FROM MEMORY AT WILL.

Looking westwards over Loch Garry towards Knoydart.

14.   ZIG-ZAGGING THROUGH THE HEAVENS

HOW MANY CLEATED SOLES HAVE PASSED

ACROSS YOUR HIGH SERRATED DYKE?

CAMPAIGNERS OLD AND NEW ALIKE

IN AWE HAVE BOWED TO YOU

GREAT NORTHERN BARRIER,

ZIG-ZAGGING THROUGH THE HEAVENS.

The Aonach Eagach Ridge, Glencoe.

15.   NICE?

*T*INY VILLAGE NESTLING

BENEATH GARGANTUAN MOUNTAINS.

IT IS SAID THEY ARE GNEISS,

BUT I SEE SOME PREHISTORIC BEAST,

WITH THE INHABITANTS

AN APERITIF, TO AN EVENING FEAST.

The village of Diabaig, Loch Torridon with Liathach behind.

16.   **AN ENCHANTED ISLAND**

I SAW THEM TOGETHER, THROUGH THE TREES,

THE SUN SMILED ON THEIR SMILES,

THEIR GAZES LONG AND MEANINGFUL.

THEY WALKED ON, AS THOUGH

THE ONLY PEOPLE ON AN ENCHANTED ISLAND.

AT CLOSER RANGE, I SAW HIS FACE,

AND THE SUN DISAPPEARED BEHIND A CLOUD.

The Island of Eigg and the Sgurr.

17.   THE MOOR OF RANNOCH

THIS DEVASTATED MOOR, ONCE NURTURED
THE GREAT FOREST OF CALEDON.
COULD IT HAVE BEEN LAST VIEWED AS AN INFERNO,
WHICH TURNED THE NIGHT TO DAY,
AWAKENED SLUMBERING SUMMITS,
AND RENDERED THE EARTH ASH-GREY?

The Clach Leathad group from the Moor of Rannoch.

18.   **THE PINNACLE**

*H*IGHER AND HIGHER THEY CLIMBED,

DRIVEN BY SOME QUEST,

NO EROSION OF RESOLVE

TILL THEY REACHED THE MOUNTAINS' CREST.

The Innaccessible Pinnacle, Sgurr Dearg, Cuillin of Skye.

20.   **EXPECTATIONS HIGH**

*N*OT LONG NOW,

ALMOST THERE,

GULLY NUMBER TWO CLOSE BY.

CONDITIONS GOOD,

BUT GRIPPING COLD,

EXPECTATIONS HIGH.

No. 2 Gully, Ben Nevis. The summit is to the left of the figures.

22. ELEPHANT HEAD

LIKE SOME SILENT MAMMOTH
ETCHED FROM AN ERA PAST.
UNLIKE YOUR HUMAN COUNTERPART,
UNMOCKED, UNRIDICULED,
AND MADE TO LAST.

Stob Coire nam Beith, Glencoe.

23.   **THE GREAT HERDSMAN**

*H*OW FINE YOU LOOK TONIGHT
IN SUMMER SOFTNESS.
A BEAUTY UNIQUE.
FINGERS OF SCREE STRETCH OUT
LIKE LIGAMENTS, JOINING
GRASS AND HEATHER,
CORRIE AND SLAB,
BELOW A PERFECT PEAK.

Buachaille Etive Mor in Summer.

24.   LAZY BEDS

*T*HEY TOILED ON THEIR LAZY BEDS,

A SOIL MIXED WITH SEAWEED.

AND UNDER A BLANKET OF CLOUD

REAPED A FRUGAL HARVEST.

Lazy beds and the Cuillin from near Carbost. (front cover)

25.   THE LITTLE RED-ROOFED HOUSE

I OFTEN SEE IT FROM ACROSS THE WATER

AT ESSAN DUBH.

THE LITTLE RED-ROOFED HOUSE,

SMALL AND REMOTE,

AS WE ARE TOO.

Loch Torridon from the north Applecross shore.

27. THE CUILLIN

*H*OW PROUD AND COMPELLING
THE CUILLIN OF SKYE.
MAGICAL WHEN MISTY,
HEAVENLY WHEN DRY.

Sgurr nan Gillean and its minions from near Sligachan.

28.   AN ELEVATED PLACE

*I*N WINTER, WARMLY CLAD SAVE FOR MY FACE,

I CLIMB THE HILL AND, FINDING SHELTER RUDE,

I LOOK OUT FROM MY ELEVATED PLACE,

TO SURVEY THE WORLD, A STILL WHITE SOLITUDE.

The peaks of Glencoe from Beinn a'Bheithir.

32.   **THE OSPREY**

*A*T SEVEN WEEKS YOU'RE FULLY GROWN.
NESTING IN SOME ISOLATED PINE.
ITS NAKED ARMS BARELY MAKE A PLINTH,
FOR YOUR TANGLED, LOFTY LABYRINTH.

An Osprey.

37. MIDGES

I LONG FOR THE RIDGES,

AWAY FROM THE MIDGES,

FOR THEY HAVEN'T A HEAD FOR THE HEIGHTS.

THEY BREED FAST IN GLEN BRITTLE,

AND THOUGH THEY ARE LITTLE,

THEY'RE LARGELY ALL ITCHING TO BITE.

Marsco and Blaven from near Sligachan, Isle of Skye.

38. **TURNING THE HAY**

THE SUN WAS STEALING AWAY,
WITH THE LAST OF ITS LIGHT
TURNING TO GOLD THE HAY,
LIGHTING CORRIE AND PEAK.
THE CROFTER, TOILING IN HIS TIMELESS WAY,
MAKING GOOD, EACH PRECIOUS MOMENT
OF THE LINGERING DAY.

Haymaking, North Ballachulish.

39.   THE OLD MILITARY BRIDGE

THIS BRIDGE WAS BUILT LONG AGO,

NEAR KINGSHOUSE HOTEL, TO THE EAST OF GLENCOE.

BUT NOW THE ENCAMPMENTS DON'T HOLD FIGHTING MEN,

JUST CLIMBERS AND WALKERS WHO VISIT THE GLEN,

QUIETLY ASSAULTING THE RIDGES,

WITH AN OCCASIONAL SWAT AT THE MIDGES.

Kingshouse Hotel, Glencoe with Buachaille Etive Mor beyond.

40. **BEACH BUBBLES**

I REMEMBER THAT NIGHT AS THOUGH IT WERE YESTERDAY.

WHITE BREAKERS ON SMOOTH WET SAND,

HAND IN HAND, A WONDERLAND, "AINT LIFE GRAND?"

YES THEY ALL APPLIED THE OLD CLICHES.

THE SAND STILL LOOKS AS SMOOTH TODAY,

BUT NOW MY HEART'S IN TUNE WITH THE BREAKING WAVES.

Rock garden, Oldshore Mor, Sutherland.

42.   **THE VENOMOUS ONE**

*H*OW CALM YOU LOOK WHEN DRAPED IN SUNSET,

AS INVITATION CALLS FROM RIDGE AND CRAG,

BUT IN THE FACE OF WINTERS ICY GRASP,

YOU'RE SCARCE A PLACE FOR EITHER MAN OR STAG.

Ben Nevis on the longest day of the year. Nevis means Venomous One.

44.   **HEADING HOME**

*H*EADING HOME WITH THE SUN.
RIDER AND HORSE AS ONE.
BOTH READY TO "HIT THE HAY",
EACH IN HIS CHOSEN WAY.

Portree harbour   *Castle Stalker, Appin.*

45.   **ON TOP**

ON TOP OF MY WORLD,
THE PAST BEHIND.
MY FUTURE UNFURLED,
IN A PURIFIED MIND.

The Cioch on a beautiful day.

46.   **EXCITEMENT**

WHEN MARCH'S BLUSTERING WIND THE LAND PREVAILS,

TREES ROCK BACK AND FORTH IN NAKED DANCE,

FULL HEDGEROWS MOVE AS ONE IN BULKING SWAY,

WITHIN, EXCITEMENT GROWS WITH EVERY GLANCE.

The peaks of Kintail.

47. SUNSET NEAR NEDD

WAVES FALL QUIETLY ON THE SHORE.

DAYLIGHT FADES

INTO DEEPENING SHADES.

AND NATURES' THRONG AND CLAMOUR IS NO MORE.

EVENSONG SPREADS,

OVER THE LAND OF NEDD.

Sunset from the road to Nedd, Sutherland.

50.   **PERFECT GLACIATION**

*H*EADING HOME IN SOLEMN MEDITATION
BETWEEN THE BUACHAILLE'S MOR AND BEAG,
I LOOK BACK ON THAT PERFECT GLACIATION,
AND FORGET MY WEARINESS OF LEG.

The Lairig Gartain, Glencoe.

51. **THE LOVERS**

$\mathcal{L}$YING TOGETHER,

SWEET CONTENTMENT

AFTER THE NEW EXPERIENCE.

A FACE PRESSED

IN THE NAPE OF A NECK.

AN ARM AROUND

A PAIR OF SMOOTH SHOULDERS.

LEGS GENTLY AND LOVINGLY INTERTWINED.

A MOULD FOREVER—IT'S MEANT TO BE.

BUT NOTHING LASTS;

A THOUGHT WHICH AT THIS MOMENT,

THEY CAN'T CONCEIVE.

En route to Sandwood Bay, Sutherland.

52.　　　　　　**A FOXGLOVE**

A FOXGLOVE IN THE EARLY LIGHT

SO VIVID BY THE LOCHSIDE

SEEMED TO TRUMPET BOLDLY

FROM ITS' SPECKLED CORE,

AND SHATTER THE SILENCE OF THE MORNING.

A foxglove at Torren Lochan, Glencoe.

53.   **THE OLD MAN** OF HOY

$\mathcal{L}$ONGSHIPS PLIED THIS RUDE COASTLINE

WHERE HAAKON BREATHED HIS LAST.

LATER, MERCHANT SHIPS

FOUNDERED ON THESE ROCKS

LIT BY "WRECKERS'" LIGHTS.

AND THE "OLD MAN" CRUMBLES

UNDER CONSTANT SIEGE.

The Old Man of Hoy, Orkney.

55.   **AMBUSH**

*T*O SEE THIS DYING BREED

CONVOYS DRIVE AT SPEED

TO A PLACE AMONG THE GORSE

AND ON ECTACHROME ENDORSE

HER SURVIVAL.

The Fort William–Mallaig steam train with Rois Bheinn behind.

56.   NOT MOTORWAY MADNESS

I'D RATHER HAVE HILLS IN DRIVING RAIN,
THAN DRIVE IN SUN IN THE FAST LANE.
WIDE OPEN SPACES, AN OPEN MIND,
FAR FROM PRESSURE OF THE WINNING KIND.

The peak of Gearr Aonach, Glencoe.

57.   **AUTUMN**

Autumn comes in ripe and russet style,

As leaves fall, summers requiem begins.

Though its sumptuous arrival makes me smile,

The parting leaves an emptiness within

Suilven from near Lochinver.

58.   **THE DYING DAY**

*I*N THE BLOOD-RED SUNSET
GLENCOE BLUSHES,
AS THE DYING DAYS'
SOFT MURMUR HUSHES.

An ethereal sunset, Glencoe.

59.   **"BY SEA, BY LAND"**

*N*OT FOR YOU A MOCK MANOEUVRE,

NO BLANKS FIRED, NO PUNCHES PULLED.

SOME REACHED LE HAVRE OR ST NAZAIRE,

SOME NEVER LEFT THESE HILLS.

The Commando Memorial, Spean Bridge.

60.   BY THE SHORES OF BALLACHULISH

*T*HE SUN SETS ON LOCH LEVEN,
BOATS ARE ANCHORED SAFE AND CALM TONIGHT.
RESTING BY THE SHORES OF BALLACHULISH,
TO WAIT THE MYSTERIES, OF DAWN'S UNFOLDING LIGHT.

Sunset, Loch Leven.

Overleaf: The Cuillin from near Sligachan

60. BY THE SHORES OF BALLACHULISH

THE SUN SETS ON LOCH LEVEN,

BOATS ARE ANCHORED SAFE AND CALM TONIGHT.

RESTING BY THE SHORES OF BALLACHULISH,

TO WAIT THE MYSTERIES, OF DAWN'S UNFOLDING LIGHT.

Sunset, Loch Leven.

Overleaf: The Cuillin from near Sligachan